Bitcoin:

Powerful Tips and Strategies for Your Trading Success

© Copyright 2017 by Christopher Baine - All rights reserved.

This document is intended to provide accurate and reliable information on the topic and problem. The publication is sold with the idea that the publisher is not required to provide accounting, officially authorized or otherwise qualified services, qualified services. If consultation is required, legal or professional, it is necessary to order a practicing specialist by profession.

In no event is it lawful to reproduce, duplicate or transmit any part of this document in electronic form or in hard copy. The recording of this publication is strictly prohibited, and any storage of this document is not allowed, unless with the written permission of the publisher. All rights reserved.

The information given herein is believed to be truthful and consistent, since any liability in terms of negligence or other use by using or abusing any policies, processes or instructions contained therein is the sole and full responsibility of the recipient reader. Under no circumstances shall any legal liability or charge be brought against the publisher for damages, damages or pecuniary damages in connection with the information contained herein, directly or indirectly.

The information here is offered for information purposes only and is of a universal nature.

Table of Contents

Introduction 1

Chapter One: The Bitcoin Trading 4

Chapter Two: What you need to know about buying and using bitcoins 9

Chapter Three: How to buy bitcoins 18

Chapter Four: tips to help you choose bitcoin-exchange 23

Chapter Five: Understanding the benefits of Bitcoin Trading 29

Chapter Six: Steps to earning a formidable income trading bitcoin 34

Chapter Seven: Why You Should Use Bitcoins 39

Chapter eight: hiring a Bitcoin broker 47

Chapter Nine: bitcoin and binary Options 55

Conclusions 61

Introduction

Technology is developing by leaps and bounds. He daily introduces new terms and systems for business and communication. The Internet has made a big contribution to this advancement; Especially when it comes to business. Currently, trading online or online currency attracts many traders. One of the most common forms of online trading is bitcoin-exchange.

Bitcoin-exchange is a new system of money for the Internet, which is working on the concept of digital currency. It initiates a system of equal payments for individuals who do not have central authority. A new concept of crypto currency, which was originally introduced in 1998, is used. Cryptography controls the creation and transaction of digital money. Bitcoin works through a software system and does not have any central controlling authority, so it is equally controlled and controlled by its users around the world.

You can work with bitcoin exchange, as well as with any other type of currency exchange. Like working with banks, it's easy to make transactions through bit-exchange. Analogues to physical trading, the user must pay for the purchase of bitcoins. The difference is that a person should open an account in some bitcoin-exchanger. The user's paid asset will be available as a digital currency, which can be used to purchase any product. Bitcoins can be exchanged with other bitcoins holders. This system works like the exchange of money in banks.

In almost all payment systems, payments can be canceled after the transaction is made through paypal or credit cards. But with bitcoins, the situation changes, since after the transaction is completed you cannot return it or cancel it. Therefore, be cautious, exchanging your bitcoins for currency environments, because you may face problems with repaying money. It is preferable to make an exchange with other bitcoins holders near you.

Benefits of Bitcoin Exchange

Bitcoin currency exchange is completely new. This is a kind of software basic payment system, where you make transactions in digital form. Here's how it can benefit you:

- Make transactions faster than other systems
- Always available for transactions
- Perform transactions without any third-party intervention
- Make transactions from anywhere in the world
- Creating more secure transactions
- Monitoring of all transactions from your home PC or smartphone
- Acquire an asset using bitcoin

Disadvantages of bitcoin

Bitcoin-exchange is an innovation in economical systems of the world. When they are practically used, there are some disadvantages. Some of them are as follows:

- Admission to the market

The number of users of bitcoins is growing, but still it is not a widely used currency or exchange system. Its level of acceptance in financial matters is still low.

- Instability

Since bitcoin is not normally used, it is not a stable currency. However, there is a hope that this instability will decrease as the list of users and the number of bitcoins on the market become more easily used.

- Partial development

The big problem is that Bitcoin software is still in the beta phase, and there are a number of imperfect functions that still need to be eliminated. New modules are under development to make bitcoins exchange safer for everyone.

Chapter One: The Bitcoin Trading

The World of Bitcoin Trading

The cost of bitcoin changes frequently and some would view the computerized resource as unstable. The truth of the matter is, however, that most monetary standards overall change in esteem a considerable amount also. What's more, individuals profit exchanging fiat monetary standards, and items, in view of these high points and low points in cost. Bitcoin exchanging and cryptographic money trades have developed a lot since the good 'ol days. There are various exchanging systems and a huge range of trades that offer different exchanging administrations. Today, we will talk about the different surroundings of the bitcoin exchanging biological system and what's in store from these trade markets.

Bitcoin Trading - The Ultimate Guide

The new digital currency made considerable progress from exchanging beneath $4 only two years back. Major on the web and disconnected retailers are beginning to include the new cash as an installment technique.

Bitcoin is a digital currency and another and one of a kind money related vehicle, not at all like anything the world has ever observed. It's known as a digital currency since it utilizes cryptography to control the creation and exchange of cash. In spite of the name, there is no physical coin whatsoever, Bitcoin is a totally electronic type of cash.

Bitcoin solves the so called "twofold spending issue" give computerized merchandise. For instance, if I have a mp3 record or a digital book on my PC, I can uninhibitedly duplicate that document a thousand times and send it to a thousand different individuals. For a computerized money, the likelihood for boundless replicating would mean a snappy hyperinflationary demise. Bitcoin solves this by keeping up a shared system and recording every exchange in an open record called the piece chain. Let's assume I send 1 bitcoin from my bitcoin deliver to my companion John. The bitcoin arrange records that exchange in the piece chain and I never again have ownership of that bitcoin. The coin ""moved"" from my bitcoin wallet to John's wallet.

What's so extraordinary about Bitcoin? There are numerous contentions on whether the new virtual cash will succeed or come up short. We won't get into this nor examine the governmental issues behind the venture. Our worry is entirely with the benefit openings given by this new installment wonder. In the following couple of pages on the new advanced cash we will layout our musings from the point of view of a broker and a potential financial specialist in this up and coming business sector.

Bitcoin Basics

Bitcoin is a shared virtual money. This implies all together for an exchange to happen, no center men or focal specialist is required. You can send any measure of bitcoins to anybody living anyplace on the planet, totally wiping out the requirement for customary outsiders like banks or cash transmitters. The cryptographic money also permits the bypassing of capital and AML limitations.

Keeping in mind the end goal to send or get bitcoins, all you need is a bitcoin address and web get to. You just should be online sufficiently long for the exchange to handle. Likewise to conventional ledgers, you can get bitcoins to your bitcoin address regardless of the possibility that you're disconnected. When you need to ""gather"" your coins however, you'll need to discover a web association.

The most effective method to get a bitcoin address

Like we said already, with a specific end goal to send or get bitcoins you should have a bitcoin address. You can get a bitcoin address either by downloading the bitcoin customer or by getting an online wallet. The two most prominent btc customers are Bitcoin-qt and Multibit. The primary difference between these two customers is in the measure of the square bind that should be downloaded. If you choose to run with Bitcoin-qt, have no less than 10 Gigabytes free space on your hard drive for the piece chain. As Bitcoin-qt is the ""authority"" bitcoin customer, if you can save 10 GB, go for this alternative. Here's a page that has well ordered guidelines on introducing Bitcoin-qt.

Multibit is a lightweight rendition of the bitcoin customer. You can read more about it here.

Where are my bitcoins stored?

But where are the bitcoins really stored? After you introduce one of the two customers above, you can discover your bitcoins in a document called wallet.dat. If you utilize windows this record will be situated in the application information area. If your PC gets stolen or lost and you haven't made a duplicate of the wallet.dat record you will lose your bitcoins. It is dependably prescribe to reinforcement this document.

The bitcoins can also be put away in online wallets. There are specific sites that offer bitcoin wallet administrations. However because of these destinations being an incessant focus for programmers, keeping bitcoins in online wallets is not suggested when you can without much of a stretch store them disconnected on your PC. Wallets can be helpful for putting away little wholes of bitcoins so that you can make snappy online buys. Some of the more well known wallet administrations are Blockchain and CoinKite.

Trades are a somewhat more secure place for your bitcoins contrasted with online wallets since they keep most coins in what is known as "chilly stockpiling". As a rule more than 90% of the bitcoins saved on a trade are kept disconnected. A little 5 to 10% save is kept nearby for quick reclamation purposes. There are a lot of aides online on the best way to store/secure bitcoins, go over them. It's constantly more secure to deal with this procedure yourself at that point to put stock in an outsider with a significant measure of bitcoins.

Bitcoin Advantages

Bitcoin has a few focal points contrasted with conventional cash transmitting administrations. We as of now said two of these over, the end of the requirement for outsiders and the bypassing of confinements.

Another major in addition to of the new cryptographic money is the minimal effort for sending and accepting bitcoins. While it is conceivable to send exchanges totally for nothing out of pocket, it is prescribed to pay the little charge keeping in mind the end goal to accelerate the sending procedure.

The expense sum relies upon the information size of the exchange. A run of the mill exchange is 500 bytes and conveys a charge of

0.0001 BTC. At current costs of $913 per bitcoin, this adds up to a charge of 9.13 pennies.

Since the charge is totally reliant on an exchange's information measure and not on the quantity of bitcoins being sent, a $10 exchange will convey an indistinguishable expense from a $10 Million exchange. The expense will take a 0.913% bit of a $10 exchange but that same charge will just take 0.000000913% of a 10 Million exchange.

Bitcoin offers advantages to vendors also, as exchanges that include the advanced cash are secure and irreversible. Without the danger of misrepresentation or false chargebacks, vendors can offer their items at a rebate in this way creating more deals or pocket the difference themselves. What's more, with card processors good and gone, traders can save money on the rate cut taken by Visa/MasterCard.

Chapter Two: What you need to know about buying and using bitcoins

Many individuals ask, 'How would I get bitcoins?'

The most straightforward and speediest approach to purchase bitcoins in a flash with a Mastercard or plastic is through Indacoin where you can secure $50 or less of bitcoin quick and more often than not inside 10 minutes.

However, you might be new to the whole cryptographic money idea and for that we suggest you take in a couple of things.

Bitcoin is to a great degree engaging but also different than the money you know and utilize each day.

Step 1 - > Get Started With Bitcoin

Before you begin utilizing Bitcoin, which is as yet test but has been operational with no intrusions for more than eight years, there are a couple of things that you have to know so as to utilize it safely and stay away from normal traps.

To begin with, Bitcoins are difficult to fake or blow up.

Second, you can utilize them to send or get any measure of cash, with anybody, anyplace on the planet, requiring little to no effort. Bitcoin installments are difficult to piece, and bitcoin wallets can't be solidified.

Third, with Bitcoin you can specifically control the cash yourself without experiencing an outsider like a bank or Paypal.

Fourth, Bitcoin exchanges can't be turned around or discounted. You should just manage organizations or individuals you trust.

Fifth, to be substantial, a Bitcoin exchanges must be affirmed at any rate once but preferably 6+ times before it has happened and ends up plainly irreversible.

Sixth, Bitcoin is not unknown but rather there is tumbling. All Bitcoin exchanges are put away freely and forever on the system, which implies anybody can see the adjust and exchanges of any Bitcoin address.

Seventh, you can get bitcoins by tolerating them as an installment for products and ventures or by getting them from a companion or someone close you. You can also get them specifically from a trade with your ledger.

Eighth, there is a developing number of administrations and vendors tolerating Bitcoin everywhere throughout the world. You can utilize Bitcoin to pay them and rate your experience to help legitimate organizations to acquire perceivability.

Ninth, the Bitcoin business is continually changing and there are numerous Bitcoin news administrations to remain up and coming.

Step 2 - > How To Get A Bitcoin Wallet

Setting up your first Bitcoin wallet is straightforward. There are a few quality portable, desktop, and half and half wallets accessible. If you need to do careful research then you can read our complete guide on the best way to locate the best Bitcoin wallet.

An extraordinary way would be:

(1) a versatile wallet like Airbitz (iPhone, Android), CoPay (iPhone, Android) or Mycelium (Android).
(2) procure bitcoins from a companion, as installment for a decent or administration or purchase bitcoins from one of the many trades.
(3) if you choose to store a lot of bitcoins and need to know they are absolutely protected at that point utilize Armory.

Best Mobile Bitcoin Wallets

iPhone and Android applications are accessible with prevalent decisions including:

wallet Copay

Copay is a Bitcoin wallet by Bitpay and accessible on iOS, Android, Windows Phone, Linux, Max OS X, and Windows. Since Copay is accessible on different stages, it's anything but difficult to utilize a similar wallet or records over numerous gadgets.

Copay's straightforward, clean UI settles on it a decent decision for new Bitcoin clients. Copay is also a decent choice for organizations because of a common record highlight, which requires a specific number of clients to sign every exchange. Two fellow benefactors, for instance, could make a 2 of 2 wallet where both will be required to sign every exchange.

wallet breadwallet (Android)

Breadwallet begun as the most well known wallet for iPhone, and now it is also accessible for Adroid gadgets running Android 6.0 or higher. The effortlessness and simple to-utilize security makes it an extraordinary place to begin for clients who are new to bitcoin.

wallet Airbitz

AirBitz is another Bitcoin wallet that is awesome for regular utilize. It's coordinated with Fold, which means you can get 20% rebates at Starbucks from inside the wallet.

Airbitz oversees accounts with usernames and passwords, but doesn't approach your assets. This sort of record creation is less demanding for less specialized clients who may experience difficulty going down or understanding HD seeds.

wallet breadwallet (iOS)

Breadwallet's blend of effortlessness and security has made it the most prominent iOS wallet. iPhone clients looking for their first Bitcoin wallet should discover Breadwallet straightforward.

Best Bitcoin Software Wallets

Bitcoin software wallets are downloaded to your PC, give you more control and don't rely upon outsider administrations. Most software bitcoin wallets require a day or so to download the blockchain before they are prepared for utilize.

wallet Armory

Arsenal is the most develop, secure and full highlighted Bitcoin wallet but it can be mechanically scary for clients. Regardless of whether you are an individual putting away $1,000 or foundation putting away $1,000,000,000 this is the most secure alternative accessible. Clients are in entire control all Bitcoin private keys and would setup be able to a safe disconnected marking process in Armory.

wallet Bitcoin Core

Bitcoin Core is the "authority" Bitcoin customer and wallet, however isn't utilized by numerous because of moderate rates and an absence of components. Bitcoin Core, however, is a full hub, which means it verifies and transmit other Bitcoin exchanges over the system and stores a duplicate of the whole blockchain. This offers better security since Core doesn't need to depend on information from outer servers or different companions on the system. Bitcoin Core steered through Tor is viewed as one of the most ideal approaches to utilize Bitcoin secretly.

Best Hybrid Bitcoin Wallets

Crossover Bitcoin enable you to both control the private keys and have the simple of utilization of a web wallet.

Copay is a Bitcoin wallet by Bitpay and accessible on iOS, Android, Windows Phone, Linux, Max OS X, and Windows. Since Copay is accessible on different stages, it's anything but difficult to utilize a similar wallet or records over numerous gadgets.

Copay's basic, clean UI settles on it a decent decision for new Bitcoin clients. Copay is also a decent choice for organizations because of a common record include, which requires a specific number of clients to sign every exchange. Two prime supporters, for instance, could make a 2 of 2 wallet where both will be required to sign every exchange.

Best Bitcoin Web Wallets

Bitcoin web wallets are the least demanding and most helpful to utilize but are conceivably less secure than the above choices in light of the fact that the private keys to your bitcoins are typically held by an outsider.

Because of the vast number of security breaks where individuals have lost bitcoins, we don't prescribe any of the current Bitcoin web wallets. A wallet like Copay can be utilized on versatile and desktop. It gives the advantages of a software wallet and is anything but difficult to use crosswise over numerous gadgets. Copay also encourages you safely share wallets with other individuals.

Best Bitcoin Hardware Wallets

Bitcoin equipment wallets are the most secure on the grounds that they don't uncover your private keys to the system.

Step 3 - > How To Get Bitcoins

The most effective method to purchase Bitcoins

With the Bitcoin value so unpredictable many individuals appear to be interested about getting some. Underneath we have recorded some of the best trades.

If you need to do your own particular research at that point check our guide on the most proficient method to purchase bitcoins in any nation. Here are our proposals:

logo Coinbase Buy

Coinbase is one of the world's biggest Bitcoin trades. Clients in the United States, Canada, the greater part of Europe, and Singapore can purchase bitcoins with an associated financial balance or SEPA exchange.

European clients can buy bitcoins with 3D secure credit or check cards.

The most effective method to Earn Bitcoins

Many individuals find that the most ideal approach to get bitcoins is to acknowledge them as installment for the items or administrations they as of now offer. Simply give your clients the alternative to pay in bitcoin.

To make it simple, you might need to agree to accept a bitcoin vendor account which enables you to send solicitations and incorporate bitcoin installments into your request pages for the most well known web based shopping basket frameworks.

What Is Bitcoin Mining?

Mining bitcoins requires an interest in specific bitcoin mining equipment intended to handle twofold round sha256 hash verifications at rapid.

Beginning with Bitcoin mining can be an overwhelming attempt and it has turned out to be profoundly specific so you might need to abandon it to experts with Bitcoin cloud mining administrations.

By the by, there are numerous amazing bitcoin mining frameworks accessible.

It is vital to bring up that bitcoin mining is profoundly focused and dangerous for would-be members. If it's not too much trouble see our bitcoin digging guide for more detail.

If you need to attempt your fortunes at bitcoin mining then this Bitcoin digger is likely the best arrangement.

Step 4 - > How To Use Bitcoins?

Beginning to utilize bitcoins can be energizing since it is another innovation. Bitcoins can be utilized to buy pretty much anything you need. Dental administrations, a shiny new auto, travel and even extravagance land.

We suggest looking the Bitcoin dealer indexes underneath to find the shippers you are occupied with. You can purchase gift cards with bitcoin and shop effectively at the vast majority of the stores you as of now utilize.

One of the best things to purchase with Bitcoin is virtual private system (VPN) administrations to protect your Internet movement, secure and private. We set up together an extensive rundown of VPNs you can purchase with Bitcoin.

Another apparatus many individuals jump at the chance to purchase is a Bitcoin plastic which empowers individuals to stack a platinum card with reserves by means of bitcoins.

Is it accurate to say that you are a vendor or specialist that would need to begin tolerating bitcoins for merchandise or administrations? We have a couple of high resolution designs that can help you.

Simply that it is in completely versatile PSD frame so notwithstanding exploding it to tremendous printable resolutions will do no mischief to them. Also, you can alter them effectively.

Gold Version

More energizing. Same arrangement: PSD and resolutions accessible without any copyrights to stress over by utilizing and modifying a current coin outline. Scaling the PSD up over 500% is fine but after that it might get hazy.

Charity

BitGive - a non-benefit establishment that is tolerating gifts from the Bitcoin people group and giving altruistic gifts to natural and general wellbeing causes around the world.

Chapter Three: How to buy bitcoins

How To Buy Bitcoins Using Coinbase

Coinbase has a pretty intuitive website which makes it pretty easy to buy Bitcoins from. Start off by signing up to Coinbase. After signing up go to "payment methods" and choose "add a bank account." Coinbase currently supports 25 countries.

After you've entered your bank account, you'll be asked to verify your account. You can do this is one of two ways:

1. Get billed for two small amounts (up to $1). After you see these amounts in your bank statement, you can just fill them in and get verified. This takes about two days and can be somewhat annoying, but it's much safer than the other option.
2. Supply Coinbase with your customer number and access code so they can verify you own this bank account. Keep in mind that your access code IS NOT YOUR PIN. If you don't know how to get your access code just Google your bank's name and "access code" and you'll probably see how in a second. Here's an example for getting an access code with Capital One.

After you verify your bank account, you will need to verify your phone number as well. Once you finish your account verification just go to "Buy Bitcoin," enter the amount you wish to buy and

click the "Buy Bitcoin" button at the bottom.

How To Buy Bitcoins Using Circle

(International credit card needed)

The circle is one of the hottest new startups at the moment which allow you to buy Bitcoins with a credit card pretty easily. The company just came out of Beta, and they claim to operate in the US. However numerous users (including myself) have managed to purchase Bitcoins through them using an international credit card even though they do not reside in the US.

First, sign up for Circle:

After you finish the signup process go to "Add funds" and deposit money into your account using your credit card.

If you didn't add a credit card on sign-up, you would be asked to do so during this step.

You should see the money in your account instantly. Once the money is in the account, you can withdraw it to your Bitcoin wallet in the form of BTC. Go to "Send money" -> click on the

"USD" sign and it will convert into BTC. Then just fill out your Bitcoin address and the amount you want to withdraw.

How to buy Bitcoins using CoinMama

(No verification needed up to $500, worldwide)

CoinMama specializes in Bitcoin purchases through a credit card. They take a premium fee for their services, but they do not limit you to a maximum amount of Bitcoins that you can buy. You can buy up to $500 worth of Bitcoin without verification. Another good feature CoinMama offers is that once you place your order with them, your price is reserved. So if the Bitcoin price goes up while you are purchasing, your price remains the same until you finish the payment process and you will be unaffected. From Coinmama's homepage, you can choose how many Bitcoins you'd like to buy/sell. You can enter the price either in BTC or USD or choose one of the offered packages.

Once finished, click "Buy Bitcoins, " and you will be taken to the sign-up page. After you fill out your initial details, you will need to go through additional verification by submitting a photo ID document. Verification is usually pretty quick (it took me 1.5 hours to get verified). You can also buy up to $500 without doing the verification process. Once verified you could buy Bitcoins pretty easily with your credit card through the simple interface. If you verified your address, I suggest you use "Visa, MasterCard via Simplex" since it's the fastest option. If you want to continue without verification, you can use the "MoneyGram" option. You can then pay the amount with your credit card on MoneyGram's website (this applies to US residents only).

The next step will be to enter your Bitcoin address. Unlike other exchanges, CoinMama doesn't keep your Bitcoins on their wallet (which is a good thing). This means you'll need to get

a Bitcoin wallet before continuing.

The last step will be to enter your payment details and place your order.

Coinmama uses the services of Simplex, allowing merchants to sell Bitcoins via credit cards as a payment method. I'll probably be doing a more in-depth review of Coinmama soon, as it has become quite a popular method for buying Bitcoins.

How to buy Bitcoins using Coin.MX

(Verification needed, worldwide, $5 bonus on first deposit)

Coin.MX is a marketplace for Bitcoins. Prices are around 1.3% higher than what you would find in Coinbase, and you will also have to go through a user verification process to deposit money. All in all, this is probably the simplest solution for buying with a credit card. If you're a first time customer at Coin.MX you'll get a $5 deposit bonus in your account.

User verification takes around 48 hours and requires uploading a short video of you holding a readable government issued document (e.g. passport). Once you've been verified, depositing funds is pretty simple and easy – just go to "deposit" and add your credit card details and you're able to buy Bitcoins.

Withdrawing your Bitcoins is pretty easy as well – keep in mind that there's a 0.001BTC withdrawal fee required. Just go to "Deposit," select "BTC" and paste your Bitcoin address. You can read my full CoinMX review here.

Below are five golden rules which you should follow in ANY Bitcoin purchasing process. I hope you enjoyed this guide and felt free to ask any questions in the comments section below or by subscribing to our blog.

Rule #1 – Check the credibility of your Bitcoin seller

When buying from an individual, validate their reputation by reviewing their trader profile if one is available. Ask for a Facebook, LinkedIn or any other social network profile to ascertain there's an actual person behind the screen. As a rule of thumb, never buy Bitcoins from someone who you cannot account for their credibility.

If you're buying at an exchange, check for the exchange name and the word "reviews." Looking for reviews about exchanges and even individuals in the Bitcointalk forum can also provide valuable insights.

Rule #2 – Document everything

Since Bitcoin is somewhat untraceable like cash, in the case of fraud, it will be hard to prove specific allegations. Make sure you document your communication with the seller in a way that will be easy to present if needed later on.

Rule #3 – when dealing with individuals: Wait for confirmation before paying

For small to the medium transaction, it's recommended to wait for at least one confirmation before submitting your payment. For larger transactions, wait for at least six confirmations.

Rule #4 – Use escrow when needed

When conducting large transactions with individuals, use a Bitcoin escrow service to hold on to your funds until you receive the required amount of confirmations. This way your money will be

in the custody of a trusted 3rd party until you receive the Bitcoins.

Rule #5 – NEVER leave your money at an exchange

If you're buying Bitcoins at an exchange, make sure to move your Bitcoins to your private Bitcoin wallet the moment you get them. NEVER leave Bitcoins inside an exchange; this can result in the loss of your Bitcoins due to theft or fraud.

Chapter Four: tips to help you choose bitcoin-exchange

In the present era of cryptocurrency, a digital currency like Bitcoin is something that every other individual is familiar with. Making use of this digital currency requires choosing a bitcoin exchange in the first place. Some people are unfamiliar with the conspicuous elements which are to be taken into consideration before choosing a bitcoin exchange and end up making the wrong decision. Taking this into consideration, we have taken the liberty of mentioning a few of the elements that you must take into consideration while choosing the bitcoin exchange.

The first and the foremost thing that you have to look for in a bitcoin exchange is the country that it is located in. It is a commendable idea to make sure that the bitcoin exchange you are choosing is located in your country. It makes the operations considerably simpler and convenient. However, provided that you are choosing an exchange that is located outside your country, you must ensure that the exchange you have chosen is dealing in the currency that you are looking for. Only then you can more ahead and look for the other elements of the bitcoin exchange.

Now comes the part of actually utilizing a bitcoin exchange to purchase the bitcoins. Before you end up finalizing your decision, it is advised to take a good look at the fees associated with the purchase to ensure that it was reasonable and by no means extravagant or unaffordable. Provided that the condition is being fulfilled, thoroughly analyze the process of purchasing to make sure that it is completely transparent. The addresses should be mentioned vividly, bitcoin reserves should be verified, and audit information should be available.

Bitcoins are not easy for people to acquire. If you're able to objectively evaluate a few things before deciding on one, you might be better off than choosing the exchange that has the best-looking website.

Let's cycle through some of the characteristics you need to consider when choosing an exchange.

Liquidity

Because Bitcoin is traded on a market where people are both looking to purchase or sell the currency, it's important to take into account the amount of liquidity that an exchange has. Liquidity is the ability to sell without the price being significantly affected, causing the price to drop. The more buyers and sellers there are the more liquidity that exists. So, what method can you use to tell how much liquidity an exchange has? One word: volume. Take a look at the top exchanges by trading volume as calculated by Bitcoincharts.

Those 30-day numbers represent the total number of Bitcoins that have been traded on each exchange. And while Mt. Gox has had its share of problems, many of them can be attributed to its growing pains. Mt.Gox is by far the largest exchange, and it very often offers the highest selling price for Bitcoins. This creates a network effect that allows them to become larger and larger as more people join that exchange.

Fees

The process of buying and selling Bitcoins costs money – that's the incentive for exchanges to be run as businesses. However, unlike buying a stock or bond, Bitcoin exchanges are in the practice of charging a percentage. This is in contrast to discount brokerages commonly used by investors in the US that charge a flat rate fee. Because of the percentage model, buying and selling Bitcoins over time can get very expensive.

This fee schedule from Bitstamp is a common structure for Bitcoin exchanges. They will often charge a higher percentage fee on a sliding scale that is based on volume. The more volume that you trade per a thirty day period, the less percentage that the exchange charges. This can be challenging for conducting many transactions since one would need to calculate percentages constantly to factor in the mathematics of trades. But the exchanges make a lot of money this way, and until an exchange with high volume starts charging flat-rate commissions – a kind of "discount Bitcoin brokerage" – this is the way that things will be.

Proximity

Bitcoin is still a relatively unregulated currency, but that is going to change over the long run. As there is more exposure in the media and financial industries regarding Bitcoin, governments will inevitably want to exert a degree of control over it as a transmission of monetary value. This is because they want to ensure that it does not become an instrument for illegal activities. Money laundering, terrorism, and illegal drug smuggling are a few of the reasons why authorities have an interest in monitoring Bitcoins.

Because of this, it is important to consider the geographic location of a Bitcoin exchange before you choose one. The location that the exchange decides to do business in will dictate what laws it will have to comply with. Most countries have not even issued guidance on Bitcoin activities like the United States' Financial Crimes Enforcement Network (FinCEN) has, but if and when many of them start to do it, it could affect your ability to transact in Bitcoins. If you have familiarity with a particular country's financial laws and regulations, you should probably pick an exchange that does business there.

Accessibility

An unfortunate reality for Bitcoin at present day is the risk of exchanges being attacked. The purpose of doing this is to change the perception of Bitcoins to profit from price swings. Bitcoin is volatile, and an attack that causes the price to drop is something that malicious hackers can profit from. This has affected the top exchange, Mt. Gox, significantly this year to the point that in April they released specific information about what they are experiencing.

One tool that can be used to measure a site's accessibility is something called host-tracker. Simply enter in the exchange URL you wish to check, and the tool will try to access it from different hosting partners around the world. You can even set up email or SMS alerts that will allow you to track a site's uptime over a period. Accessibility to an exchange is obviously important; you have to factor in an exchange's risk of being attacked for monetary reasons in your decisions to choose one.

If you've made the decision to purchase Bitcoins, you also have to make a choice about which exchange to use. This is something that should be done with some considerations in mind. Not all exchanges are made equal, and everyone has a special set of circumstances. Because of this, it is important to think about liquidity, fees, proximity, and accessibility as well as your situation when choosing an exchange.

Good Security:

Major Bitcoin exchanges face hacking attempts every day. Even leading exchanges have suffered leaks in the past. It's part of dealing with some of the most talented hackers in the world. Nevertheless, you'll want a Bitcoin exchange with strong security and a limited history of leaks.

Your Privacy:

One of the best parts about buying Bitcoins is that you can do it with 100% privacy. However, the only real way to privately buy Bitcoins is with cash or a cash deposit. Not all exchanges support this. It's easy to find exchanges that accept bank transfers, credit card payments, debit card payments, and PayPal, for example. However, each of these payment methods is tied to your personally-identifiable information. If you want to avoid being tracked, then you need an exchange that offers cash or cash deposit exchanges.

It would be a commendable idea to take a look at the processing time of your purchase with the chosen bitcoin exchange. Remember that it should not be an unreasonably time-consuming process. The faster the exchange, the more reliable it is. A few of the bitcoin exchanges does also enable you to keep a major portion of your anonymity as well, however, keeping complete anonymity isn't exactly going to be possible as long as you are making use of an online bitcoin exchange. Moreover, before finalizing the decision of choosing a bitcoin exchange, making an extensive research online to get to know the general reputation of the exchange is going to help a great deal in ensuring that you don't end up making a bad decision.

In the light of the information mentioned above, it can almost be taken for granted that choosing a bitcoin exchange is one of the essential parts of joining the world of cryptocurrency. There are some different things which are to be taken into consideration before finalizing the decision of choosing a particular bitcoin exchange. Provided that you have analyzed each one of them thoroughly, then only you can prevent all kinds of unnecessary complications associated with a particular exchange. It may take a bit of your time, but it is going to be worth it.

Chapter Five: Understanding the benefits of Bitcoin Trading

Bitcoin is a peer-to-peer network and digital currency first introduced in 2009. It is decentralized and independent of any government or banking authorities. Among other benefits, bitcoin allows users the option to make financial transactions at lower fees than the traditional online payment mechanisms.

As a user, bitcoins are helpful in facilitating financial transactions with minimal fees. Available to both regular and new users looking to invest in Bitcoin, all users are able to buy or sell Bitcoin from established Bitcoin exchanges. Since bitcoins can be converted into a number of different fiat currencies, companies such as Wirex offer users a seamless method of converting your bitcoins into fiat money, and vice versa. Bitcoins enable you to make transactions to merchants for goods purchases, which makes it an enticing opportunity to those who believe Bitcoin has a bright future.

Why invest in bitcoin?

The key reason for bitcoin's attractiveness to investors is the volatility it has seen in its early years.

In late 2013, investors enthusiastically took to bitcoin as a vehicle for investment. Bitcoin took off in a big way, increasing massively in value from $200 per bitcoin in November 2013 to over $1000 a month later.

Since then, bitcoin's price has seen huge levels of volatility. There are two key reasons for this:

Scarcity of supply

Firstly, bitcoin still has a relatively small number of total coins in circulation. Because of how bitcoin is designed, a certain number of bitcoins are released every ten minutes until the maximum 21 million are in circulation. That point will only be reached in 2140, so volatility is a key feature in bitcoin's early years.

Early days

Secondly, bitcoin is still facing questions surrounding its legitimacy and security. As investors and adopters fear a major government taking decisive action against the currency, any signs that government figures are considering regulation can impact its price. Major scandals surrounding bitcoin were rife for much of 2014 and beyond, with the collapse of Mt. Gox and Bitstamp amongst other troubles.

Offers Several Uses

Initially, users were introduced to bitcoins as a digital currency to carry out routine financial transactions with minimal charges, when compared to other forms of online payment sources. However, since then, it has emerged that there is a vast array of other uses for bitcoins that users have come to learn as the market began maturing. Bitcoin utilizes blockchain technology to facilitate digital transactions, where all transactions are recorded and held for the verification purposes to process them further based on their validity. All transactions are public ledger and viewable online through the Blockchain website. Other activities that can be done through the bitcoins include digital trading of securities; for land titles and other property; for insurance claims; as a payment rail for remittances; for settlement between financial institutions; for document stamping and auditing, for customer rewards and crowdfunding, and much more.

Each of these Bitcoin uses is still in the early stages of development, and so they might take time to become mainstream. However, the success in even one of these transactions may be significant enough to induce a big revolution in the industry and will rapidly increase in value. So, it is worth investing in BTC, and it will give you good returns in the long run along with the starting benefits of having smooth digital financial transactions at a low price.

Expected Gains Are More Than Expected Losses

The potential gain in BTC is more than the potential loss; and this is because several crypto-analysts have speculated that bitcoin could become a global currency in the future though it is very hypothetical. If this becomes reality, then it will stimulate international trade all around the world. In turn, economists have speculated that the price would hike to 20,000 times its value, which will make each $1 worth of current BTC would (hypothetically) be worth $20,000 in the future. However, this will only happen if bitcoin was recognized as legal tender for both international and domestic trade. This forecast is one made by experts who believe that investing in bitcoin will deliver a $200 return for each dollar you invest. Though this is just a prediction and it still remains a relatively risky investment owing to its decentralized nature, it is not impossible to expect these kinds of profits because the rewards are expected to be higher when trading commodities.

Provides Interest On Your Investment

Bitcoin is considered as commodity money, so when you hold bitcoins, you can invest them in the same way you might invest in a business with fiat money. Like fiat currency, you'll generate interest on this investment as well, so holding some Bitcoins can allow you to invest them and earn interest on the same. Moreover, you can receive good returns at increased prices on your investment too as time elapses.

Easy Access

With Bitcoins, you are not required to tie your money up in long-term plans to make a profit and you can make a profit in a short space of time depending on how much money is being transferred through the Bitcoin network. As such, you can simply invest in them and use the interest generated for your daily transactions like purchasing groceries, which means you get instant access to your money for your financial transactions even though it's invested.

In short, buying Bitcoins in 2017 will appear to be a good move for some as it is likely to further increase in value and popularity, so it's worth keeping an eye on its development throughout the year for a great investment opportunity.

Quick and Cheap Transactions

When making a Bitcoin transfer the fees are extremely low compared to conventional methods of moving money. A normal Bitcoin fee is 0.0005 BTC per transfer (0.2 THB, less than a 25 satang coin), whereas with a typically international wire transfer you could expect to pay 700THB-1300THB per transaction. Accepting credit cards will generally cost 3-5% of the transfer amount, which again is much more expensive than a Bitcoin transaction.

International wire transfers can take from a few days to more than a week, whereas Bitcoin transactions are generally confirmed with an hour.

Irreversible Transactions

As existing merchants will be well aware, when accepting credit card payments, or even bank payments the sender has the ability to reverse or "chargeback" the payment. There is nothing worse than sending products to a customer, only to receive a message that the payment has been reversed, you have been cheated and there is nothing you can do about it.

Bitcoin is the only payment method that is 100% irreversible and cannot be charged back. For this reason you should be careful when sending Bitcoins; be sure that you are sending them to a trusted vendor.

No Paperwork

Anyone, from any country, of any age can accept Bitcoins within minutes. There is no ID card, passport or proof of address that all conventional banks required to open an account. All you need to do to start sending and receiving Bitcoins is to download a Bitcoin Wallet program and generate a Bitcoin Address.

You could have 1000s of different addresses if you wanted, there is no limit to the number of Bitcoin Addresses that you can have.

Appreciating Value

As you can see from the Bitcoin exchange value graph shown on our homepage, the value of Bitcoins were initially highly volatile during the first few years of it's inception, however during the last 6 months the currency has stabilized and has been steadily increasing in value on a daily basis.

Chapter Six: Steps to earning a formidable income trading bitcoin

Step 1 - Understanding Bitcoin And The Block-Chain

Bitcoin is a shared installment framework, also called electronic cash or virtual money. It offers a twenty-first century contrasting option to physical managing an account. Trades are made by means of "e wallet programming". The bitcoin has really subverted the conventional managing an account framework, while working outside of government controls.

Bitcoin utilizes cutting edge cryptography, can be issued in any fragmentary section, and has a decentralized circulation framework, is sought after all around and offers a few unmistakable favorable circumstances over different monetary standards, for example, the US dollar. For one, it can never be embellished or solidified by the bank(s) or an administration office.

In 2009, when the bitcoin was worth only ten pennies for each coin, you would have transformed a thousand dollars into millions, in the event that you held up only eight years. The quantity of bitcoins accessible to be acquired is restricted to 21,000,000. At the time that this article was composed, the aggregate bitcoins available for use was 16,275,288, which implies that the rate of aggregate bitcoins "mined" was 77.5%. around then. The present estimation of one bitcoin, at the time that this article was composed, was $1,214.70 USD.

As indicated by Bill Gates, "Bit coin is energizing and superior to cash". Bitcoin is a de-brought together type of cash. There is no longer any need a "trusted, outsider" required with any exchanges.

By removing the banks from the condition, you are additionally disposing of the lion's offer of every exchange charge. Also, the measure of time required to move cash from indicate A point B, is diminished impressively.

The biggest exchange to ever occur utilizing bitcoin is one hundred and fifty million dollars. This exchange occurred in seconds with insignificant fee's. With a specific end goal to exchange substantial totals of cash utilizing a "trusted outsider", it would take days and cost hundreds if not a huge number of dollars. This clarifies why the banks are viciously contradicted to individuals purchasing, offering, exchanging, exchanging and spending bitcoins.

Only .003% of the universes (250,000) populace is evaluated to hold no less than one bitcoin. What's more, just 24% of the populace recognize what it is. Bitcoin exchanges are entered sequentially in a "blockchain" simply the way bank exchanges are. Pieces, in the mean time, resemble singular bank explanations. At the end of the day, blockchain is an open record of all Bitcoin exchanges that have ever been executed. It is continually developing as "finished" pieces are added to it with another arrangement of recordings. To utilize traditional saving money as a similarity, the blockchain resembles a full history of managing an account exchanges.

Step 2 - Setting Up Your E Wallet Software Account

When you make your own particular interesting e wallet programming account, you will be able to exchange reserves from your e wallet to a beneficiaries e wallet, as bitcoin. In the event that you might want to utilize a bitcoin ATM to pull back assets from your record, basically you will connect your e wallet "address" to the picked ATM machines e wallet 'address'. To encourage the exchange of your assets in bitcoin to and from an exchanging stage, you will basically interface your e wallet "address" to the e wallet "address" of your picked exchanging stage. In reality, it is considerably less demanding than it sounds. The expectation to learn and adapt in connection to utilizing your e wallet, is short.

To set up an e wallet, there are a heap of organization's online that offer sheltered, secure, free and turn-key e-wallet arrangements. A basic Google pursuit will enable you to locate the correct e wallet programming for you, contingent on what your necessities are precisely. Many individuals begin utilizing a "blockchain" account. This is allowed to set up and exceptionally secure. You have the alternative of setting up a two-level login convention, to additionally improve the wellbeing and security, in connection to your e wallet account, basically shielding your record from being hacked into.

There are numerous choices with regards to setting up your e wallet. A decent place to begin is with an organization called QuadrigaCX. You would find be able to them by doing a Google look. Quadrigacx utilizes the absolute most stringent security conventions that as of now exist. Besides, Bitcoins that are subsidized in QuadrigaCX are put away in frosty capacity, utilizing the absolute most secure cryptographic systems conceivable. At the end of the day, it is an exceptionally safe place for your bitcoin and other computerized monetary forms.

Keeping in mind the end goal to pull back cash in your nearby money, from your e wallet, you are required to find a bitcoin ATM, which can regularly be found in neighborhood organizations inside most significant urban areas. Bitcoin ATM's can be situated by doing a straightforward Google look.

Step 3 - Purchase Any Fractional Denomination Of Bitcoin

To purchase any measure of bitcoin, you are required to manage an advanced cash representative. Likewise with any money dealer, you should pay the expedite a charge, when you buy your bitcoin. It is conceivable to buy .1 of bitcoin or less if that is all that you might want to buy. The cost is basically in light of the present market estimation of a full bitcoin at any given time.

There are a horde of bitcoin agents on the web. A straightforward Google hunt will enable you to effortlessly source out the best one for you. It is dependably a smart thought to contrast their rates earlier with continuing with a buy. You ought to likewise affirm the rate of a bitcoin on the web, before making a buy through an intermediary, as the rate tends to vary every now and again.

Step 4 - Stay Away From Any Trading Platfrom Promising Unrealistic Returns To Unsuspecting Investors

Finding a trustworthy bitcoin exchanging organization that offers an exceptional yield is fundamental to your online achievement. Acquiring 1% every day is viewed as an exceptional yield in this industry. Winning 10% every day is outlandish. With online bitcoin exchanging, it is attainable to twofold your advanced cash inside ninety days. You should abstain from being attracted by any organization that is putting forth returns, for example, 10% every day. This sort of an arrival is not practical with advanced money exchanging. There is an organization called Coinexpro that was putting forth 10% every day to bitcoin merchants. Furthermore, it wound up being a ponzi plot. In the event that it's 10% every day, leave. The previously mentioned exchanging stage seemed, by all accounts, to be extremely modern and appeared to be being true blue. My recommendation is to concentrate on exchanging your bitcoin with an organization that offers sensible returns, for example, 1% every day. There will be different organizations that will endeavor to isolate you from your bitcoin utilizing deceitful strategies. Be extremely careful with regards to any organization that is putting forth farfetched returns. When you exchange your bitcoin to a beneficiary, there is actually nothing your can do to get it back. You should guarantee that your picked exchanging organization is completely computerized and incorporated with blockchain, from receipt to installment. All the more imperatively, it is vital that you figure out how to separate honest to goodness exchanging openings from corrupt "company's" that are specialists with regards to isolating it's customers from their cash. The bitcoin and other advanced monetary standards are not the issue. It is the exchanging stages that you should practice alert with, before giving over your well deserved cash.

Your ROI ought to likewise be upwards of 1%+ every day on the grounds that the exchanging organization that you are loaning your bitcoin to, is no doubt procuring upwards of 5%+ every day, by and large. Your ROI should likewise be consequently moved into your "e-wallet" at consistent interims, all through your agreement term. There is just a single stage that I feel great utilizing. It pay's each bitcoin financial specialist/broker 1.1% every day in enthusiasm and 1.1% every day in capital. This sort of an arrival is stunning contrasted with what you would gain with conventional money related markets, in any case, with digital money, it is normal. Most banks will payout 2% every year!

In the event that you are required to direct dreary exercises, for example, signing into your record, sending messages, tapping on joins and so on, you unquestionably need to continue looking for a reasonable exchanging organization that offers a set-it-and-overlook it sort of stage, as they completely exist.

Chapter Seven: Why You Should Use Bitcoins

Bitcoin is a relatively new form of currency that is just beginning to hit the mainstream, but many people still don't understand why they should make the effort to use it.

Why use bitcoin? Here are good reasons why it's worth taking the time to get involved in this virtual currency.

It's fast

When you pay a cheque from another bank into your bank, the bank will often hold that money for several days, because it can't trust that the funds are really available. Similarly, international wire transfers can take a relatively long time. Bitcoin transactions, however, are generally far faster.

Transactions can be instantaneous if they are "zero-confirmation" transactions, meaning that the merchant takes on the risk of accepting a transaction that hasn't yet been confirmed by the bitcoin blockchain. Or, they can take around 10 minutes if a merchant requires the transaction to be confirmed. That is far faster than any inter-bank transfer.

It's cheap

What's that you say? Your credit card transactions are instantaneous too? Well, that's true. But your merchant (and possibly you) pay for that privilege. Some merchants will charge a fee for debit card transactions too, as they have to pay a 'swipe fee' for fulfilling them. Bitcoin transaction fees are minimal, or in some cases free.

Central governments can't take it away

Remember what happened in Cyprus in March 2013? The Central Bank wanted to take back uninsured deposits larger than $100,000 to help recapitalize itself, causing huge unrest in the local population. It originally wanted to take a percentage of deposits below that figure, eating directly into family savings. That can't happen with bitcoin. Because the currency is decentralized, you own it. No central authority has control, and so a bank can't take it away from you. For those who find their trust in the traditional banking system unravelling, that's a big benefit.

There are no chargebacks

Once bitcoins have been sent, they're gone. A person who has sent bitcoins cannot try to retrieve them without the recipient's consent. This makes it difficult to commit the kind of fraud that we often see with credit cards, in which people make a purchase and then contact the credit card company to make a chargeback, effectively reversing the transaction.

People can't steal your payment information from merchants

This is a big one. Most online purchases today are made via credit cards, but in the 1920s and '30s, when the first precursors to credit cards appeared, the Internet hadn't yet been conceived. Credit cards were never supposed to be used online and are insecure. Online forms require you to enter all your secret information (the credit card number, expiry date, and CSV number) into a web form. It's hard to think of a less secure way to do online business. This is why credit card numbers keep being stolen.

Bitcoin transactions, however, don't require you to give up any secret information. Instead, they use two keys: a public key, and a private one. Anyone can see the public key (which is actually your bitcoin address), but your private key is secret. When you send a bitcoin, you 'sign' the transaction by combining your public and private keys together, and applying a mathematical function to them. This creates a certificate that proves the transaction came from you. As long as you don't do anything silly like publishing your private key for everyone to see, you're safe.

It isn't inflationary

The problem with regular fiat currency is that governments can print as much of it as they like, and they frequently do. If there are not enough US dollars to pay off the national debt, then the Federal Reserve can simply print more. If the economy is sputtering, then the government can take newly created money and inject it into the economy, via a much-publicised process known as quantitative easing. This causes the value of a currency to decrease.

If you suddenly double the number of dollars in circulation, then that means there are two dollars where before there was only one. Someone who had been selling a chocolate bar for a dollar will have to double the price to make it worth the same as it was before, because a dollar suddenly has only half its value. This is called inflation, and it causes the price of goods and services to increase. Inflation can be difficult to control, and can decrease people's buying power. Bitcoin was designed to have a maximum number of coins. Only 21 million will ever be created under the original specification. This means that after that, the number of bitcoins won't grow, so inflation won't be a problem. In fact, deflation – where the price of goods and services falls – is more likely in the bitcoin world.

It's as private as you want it to be

Sometimes, we don't want people knowing what we have purchased. Bitcoin is a relatively private currency. On the one hand, it is transparent – thanks to the blockchain, everyone knows how much a particular bitcoin address holds in transactions. They know where those transactions came from, and where they're sent. On the other hand, unlike conventional bank accounts, no one knows who holds a particular bitcoin address. It's like having a clear plastic wallet with no visible owner. Everyone can look inside it, but no one knows whose it is. However, it's worth pointing out that people who use bitcoin unwisely (such as always using the same bitcoin address, or combining coins from multiple addresses into a single address) risk making it easier to identify them online.

You don't need to trust anyone else

In a conventional banking system, you have to trust people to handle your money properly along the way. You have to trust the bank, for example. You might have to trust a third-party payment processor. You'll often have to trust the merchant too. These organizations demand important, sensitive pieces of information from you. Because bitcoin is entirely decentralized, you need trust no one when using it. When you send a transaction, it is digitally signed, and secure. An unknown miner will verify it, and then the transaction is completed. The merchant need not even know who you are, unless you've arranged to tell them.

You own it

There is no other electronic cash system in which your account isn't owned by someone else. Take PayPal, for example: if the company decides for some reason that your account has been misused, it has the power to freeze all of the assets held in the account, without consulting you. It is then up to you to jump through whatever hoops are necessary to get it cleared, so that you can access your funds. With bitcoin, you own the private key and the corresponding public key that makes up a bitcoin address. No one can take that away from you (unless you lose it yourself, or host it with a web-based wallet service that loses it for you).

You can create your own money

In spite of the amazing advances in home office colour printing technology, most national governments take a fairly dim view of you producing your own money. With bitcoin, however, it is encouraged. You can certainly buy bitcoins on the open market, but you can also mine your own if you have enough computing power. After covering your initial investment in equipment and electricity, mining bitcoins is simply a case of leaving the machine switched on, and the software running. And who wouldn't like their computer to earn them money while they sleep?

Sending money internationally

I used to live in Germany, and occasionally I will ask friends there to send me things I can't buy in the U.S. In the past, I would use Western Union to wire them money for the purchases. But if I wanted to send $100, I was slapped with a minimum fee of $5 (going as high as $25, depending on the payment method and location), not to mention Western Union's often less-than-favorable exchange rate, which further added to the cost.

Today, I use Bitcoin to send them money. With 1 percent conversion fees on either side, that adds up to about $2 in fees for a

$100 purchase. The best part is, instead of taking three to five days, my transaction is processed in only about 10 minutes.

Splitting the check

I often go out to eat with friends, and there's always an awkward pause when the bill comes. If we're lucky, the restaurant lets us split the bill four ways. Otherwise, we have to ask the server to break a bunch of twenties or figure out amongst ourselves who's paying how much now and who will have to get it the next time.

With Bitcoin, one person picks up the whole check and the rest of us pay her our portion of the meal right there from our phones. It's faster, cleaner, and a lot less cumbersome.

It's made for our generation

What we mean by that is bitcoin is made for the Internet-generation. We are quickly moving past the days of carrying around paper cash or pulling out your credit card. Bitcoin goes several steps further than the convenience of credit cards by equipping users with a payment option that is significantly lower in fees, provides virtually instantaneous transaction time, and is accessible through the dozens of bitcoin wallets.

On top of convenience, bitcoin offers credit card users freedom from the concerns of fraud, identity theft, and crippling interest rates. It's no surprise that a recent report from Goldman Sachs discovered that 33% of millennials do not think they will need a bank account in 5 years.

Bitcoin is Great for Merchants

It may feel easy to make a purchase with your credit card. You just swipe your card and receive your goods. In reality, credit card transactions are much more complex. For the merchant, a credit card transaction can take more than 60 days to be confirm with a payment processor like Visa or Mastercard. This means a merchant may not actually be able to spend the income from your purchase for 2-3 months! That's not to mention the risk of fraud and chargebacks.

Bitcoin works more like cash. If a merchant receives cash, it can feel confident that the transaction is complete. Bitcoin payments are irreversible as well, so merchants can accept Bitcoin with confidence and don't have to worry about fraud or chargebacks.

Because a digital wallet is all that's needed to receive Bitcoin, any merchant with a phone or computer can accept Bitcoin for free. There is no need to sign up with a payment processor like PayPal or Square, and 100% of the payment amount hits the merchant's pockets.

Bitcoin Payments are Secure

Each time you swipe your credit card, you must trust that the merchant accepting your payment will keep your card details secure. This is because credit card payments are pull payments: you allow a third-party to view your account details, and trust them to both debit only the correct amount and keep your information safe.

Bitcoin is the opposite: Bitcoin payments are "push" payments. The owner of bitcoins must approve each transaction, just like an email can only be sent by hitting "send". Push payments create unique use cases.

In 2013, a college student held up a Bitcoin QR code on national television. The QR code contained the student's Bitcoin address, which was now publicly available to hundreds of thousands of national viewers. These viewers opened up their Bitcoin wallets, scanned the student's QR code, and sent donations. The student received about $24,000 worth of Bitcoin. Try doing that with credit cards or bank transfers!

Bitcoin the payment system and bitcoin the currency are already making a huge impact on the world. And this may just be the beginning. The true impact of Bitcoin is unknown, and new use cases are sure to pop up as the $1 billion of venture capital poured into Bitcoin startups goes to work.

Chapter eight: hiring a Bitcoin broker

What is a Bitcoin Broker?

One of a some-more engaging developments in a universe of Bitcoin is how not everybody uses a unchanging sell to buy cryptocurrency. The supposed Bitcoin brokers have gained a lot of recognition over a past few years. Some of these platforms also support choice currencies, tokens, and digital assets. However, it seems there is still some difficulty as to how a Bitcoin attorney operates exactly.

The Inner Workings of a Bitcoin Broker

When it comes to shopping Bitcoin and other cryptocurrencies, many people automatically pointer adult for an exchange. That is usually normal, as these platforms are a "gatekeepers" to modify between fiat banking and Bitcoin. Exchanges offer business all over a world, and mostly support mixed fiat currencies. The many common exchanges embody Coinbase, Kraken, and Bithumb.

Now that scarcely each nation has the possess Bitcoin and cryptocurrency exchange, one wonders because Bitcoin brokers even exist. There is a really good reason because they are around given they yield some-more available entrance to Bitcoin and other cryptocurrencies. While they are reduction renouned than exchanges as of right now, one should never bonus a Bitcoin attorney by any means. Such services can be utterly invaluable.

Bitcoin brokers are often referred to as OTC trading services, since they offer the exact same type of functionality. Trading Bitcoin and other cryptocurrencies over the counter provides quite a few advantages. This is especially true for novice users looking to enter the world of Bitcoin. Signing up for an exchange and going through the verification process is a cumbersome endeavor, and can often take days, if not weeks to complete. Such delays often result in users not purchasing cryptocurrency in the end, as the process takes too long.

The biggest advantage a Bitcoin broker provides is how prices are less subject to price volatility. When using an exchange, users have to wait for other people to match their buy or sell orders. A Bitcoin broker, on the other hand, will sell or buy Bitcoin at a fixed price, without any arguments. While there is a premium to take into account for broker trades – often between 5% and 10% – it is a more convenient solution for people looking to buy small amounts of Bitcoin.

At the same time, using a bitcoin broker can be subject to some minor issues as well. During times of extremely high demand, it is possible brokers run out of Bitcoins to fulfill orders. This has happened to some Dutch companies not that long ago. While this is positive news for Bitcoin in general, the lack of currency to fulfill orders can be quite problematic for novice users who are not familiar with the concept of liquidity.

In the end, people who look to buy Bitcoin quickly and in a convenient manner are often better off using a broker compared to an exchange. Brokers often support additional payment methods, including credit and debit cards. For the average person on the street, that service is far superior compared to using exchanges. Bitcoin brokers certainly have their place in the ecosystem, and they will only become more popular as time progresses. A great place to find Bitcoin brokers is Localbitcoins, you can find people who will exchange Bitcoin's to cash locally in your area and can even check each one's reputation according to their trades.

How to be a Bitcoin Broker & Make Money

Many people who get hooked on digital currency become so passionate about the subject that they want to change their entire career to work in this industry. Of course there are many different ways you can go about doing that, but one of the most accessible and profitable career choices is to set yourself up as a Bitcoin broker.

Becoming a broker does require you to have some capital behind you, but if you are willing to start small in your spare time and build your business up gradually this shouldn't be a stumbling block for most people – if you have enough to buy or sell a bitcoin or two for your first trade then this may well be enough to get started. Of course if you have more than that, then things will be a lot easier for you.

The Risks of Being a Bitcoin Broker

There are three main risks associated with becoming a Bitcoin broker: the risk of being scammed, the risk of breaking the law or contravening regulations and getting prosecuted, and the risk of losing money due to fluctuating exchange rates.

Compliance: Do You Need a License to be Bitcoin Broker?

Whether or not you need to obtain a license to legally operate as a bitcoin broker is something of a disputed question. It will also depend on the legal jurisdiction in which you are operating (which includes the location of your clients as well as your own). The safest course of action for anybody considering getting into this business is to consult a legal adviser who can give you expert guidance.

If you live in the United States, for example, it is usually recommended that you obtain a 'Money Transmitter License', but with little legal precedent and regulators in individual states taking differing positions, the situation is still unclear. In many other countries, such as the UK for example, the situation is even less clear, as the government is taking a 'wait and see approach' to regulation; this usually means that people do not bother to get a license.

Being licensed usually means that you need to comply with certain requirements, such as taking the personal details of clients and keeping records for a certain amount of time.

Even in countries like the US where certain authorities state that digital currency brokerages do need a license, many trades take places on peer-to-peer websites; since ordinary users are free to buy and sell coins without registering as a business, this creates a blurred line for solo traders who are just testing the waters to get started – at which point do you cross the line from being a regular user buying and selling with other users, to becoming a brokerage business that needs to be registered? There is no hard and fast answer to questions like that and you will have to determine for yourself whether your activities may have crossed this blurred line and what your appetite for risking prosecution and fines may be.

Don't Get Scammed

Scammers do target brokers and you need to take this into consideration. When you take payment using a method through which payments can be reversed or cancelled, and in return for

Bitcoins whose transactions cannot be reversed, you are taking a risk. A customer may try to reverse a payment themselves in order to get free coins (which you can usually challenge) or they may be a criminal who pays you with a hacked account, in which case the payment processor themselves may reverse it.

To mitigate against this you need to be well versed in the policies for each of the payment methods you choose to accept and make sure that your prices reflect the comparative risk that you are taking. You can also reduce your risk by requiring ID verification from customers.

Reducing Currency Risk

A broker is often ready to either buy or sell at any time, taking a profit from the difference between bid and ask prices. This does mean, however, than you risk losing money if the price changes significantly. For example, if you buy Bitcoin with the intention of selling it, then the price falls by 20%, then it is highly unlikely that you will be able to sell it without taking a loss.

There is no way to mitigate against this 100%, so you need to make sure you are making enough profit to cover potential losses. But you can reduce the risk in the following ways:

- Reduce your trade volume or even stop trading during periods of high volatility.
- Identify trends: If you think the price is falling then reduce your buy orders or place them further from the going rate.

Peer to Peer Marketplaces

The easiest way to get started as a bitcoin broker is to use a peer-to-peer marketplace services where anybody can register and start buying and selling coins immediately. Most of these sites will allow you to choose between multiple fiat payment methods, including national bank transfers and digital wallets like Paypal or OKPay.

As both professional traders and individual bitcoiners use these sites in a very similar way there is no minimum capital requirement – as long as you have enough cash or coins to make a trade you can use a service like this, although there may be a small minimum bitcoin balance for creating your own adverts. You also don't need to go out looking for customers – you just create an offer or respond to somebody else's offer.

Of course the other side of that same coin (pun not intended) is that there is a lot of competition when you use something like this. It is also true that reputation – having an established history or trades through that particular site or service – is important. This means that beginners may have to start off by making trades with no profit, or even at a small loss, in order to build up a reputation and perhaps a few regular customers, before they can start getting any significant amount of business at more profitable prices.

The most popular peer-to-peer marketplace is LocalBitcoins. This site has a good number of users in most countries around the world, and enables trades using a wide range of different payment methods. There is also an active forum where you can network with other brokers and pick up tips and information or ask questions of more experienced traders.

Another interesting service is Multisigna. The technology behind this exchange is more advanced than local bitcoin and is more secure; because it uses multi-sig security users holding coins on the site do not take the same risk, of being hacked or of the site going out of business and taking users' balances, that you take with a centralized escrow service like LocalBitcoins. But there are fewer payment options and they have significantly fewer users as well.

'Over The Counter' Sales

Another way to operate your business is to conduct 'over the counter' sales. These are larger sales negotiated with individual buyers and sellers, rather than through placing publicly viewable offers on an exchange.

The advantages of operating like this are that you make a smaller number of larger trades, meaning more profit per trade, and that you will probably not have to pay commission to work through a third party service.

The disadvantage is that you will have to find your own clients, rather than tapping into a large and established client base through on an existing exchange.

You can set yourself up as an 'OTC' broker by creating and advertising your own website, or through using something like the Bitcoin OTC Web of Trust. Creating your own site comes with an additional opportunity to act as a broker for alternative cryptocurrencies as well as BTC.

Operating an Exchange

White label exchange services such as the one operated by Leverate allow brokers to set up their own exchange website / app with full trading platform, and even to aggregate liquidity from other exchanges.

This is a highly competitive market which will probably require a significant investment as well as a lot of work to make a success out of, but arguably offers a much greater potential profit than the other options listed here.

And Also...

The LakeBTC exchange is advertising the opportunity to become a 'LakeBanker' on their website. They give few details, however, as to exactly what this entails and what terms they are offering. When I contacted them they replied swiftly asking for more details on my personal experience and circumstances, but when I replied saying that I wanted further information for this article they didn't get back to me. I will leave it to the reader to decide if it is worth pursuing more information about this opportunity.

Chapter Nine: bitcoin and binary Options

In order to understand how the relationship between bitcoin and binary options works, we need to take a look at the history of financial trading. We should look at the evolution of money markets, financial markets and the different types of trading that we have today.

The financial markets have been evolving for thousands of years now. In earlier years you could have exchanged money with gold or silver quite easily. As time passed by this became impossible, and today you simply can't get gold from the bank worth the money that you deposit in your account. The financial market on the other hand has for a long time now been accessible to only a few investors who have knowledge about them. This has brought about a unique relationship between bitcoin and binary options.

The basics

What is binary options trading and how does it work? This is a platform where you can predict how an underlying asset, such as Google, Amazon or AT&T, will behave. You pick a strike price and place a call or a put trade and after a specified time get a payout depending on whether you were right in your prediction or not. The good thing about binary options trading is that you can trade even if you have as little as $10. The payouts are usually in the range of 70-80% if you win and 0-15% if your prediction turns out wrong.

What is a bitcoin and how does it work? This is a form of electronic currency that was created by the pseudonymous Satoshi Nakamoto. It is created and held electronically and this makes it decentralized. It has features just like traditional currencies such as the dollar, euro and yen. The difference between bitcoin and the other currencies is that bitcoins can only be traded digitally and are not held or controlled by any bank.

Unlike conventional currencies, which are based on gold and silver, bitcoins are based on an online mathematics app.

How can bitcoin be merged into binary options trading?

We have already seen that both bitcoin and binary options are new ways of doing things that deviate from the conventional path. In recent years when bitcoin started becoming popular around the world and among traders, it started to be seen as an alternative currency on several platforms. This is where binary options came in.

Binary option brokers have for a long time been presenting their customers/ traders with conventional assets, commodities and currencies such as the AUD/EUR, JPY/USD, USD/CAD and so on. With the introduction of bitcoin, several brokers saw an opportunity for their traders and introduced them to their long list of tradable currencies. It is now common to find BTC/USD, BTC/EUR and so on among the currency options being offered by different binary options brokers.

The possibilities presented by trading bullish bitcoins

Bitcoin is generally bullish. It is almost impossible to find bitcoin going down in value even when put against a high performing currency. In most instances therefore, you will find that trading bitcoin against another currency is more on the bullish side than the bearish one. Here are the options you have when you decide to trade using bitcoin;

1. As an investment currency – The first option is to open an account with a binary options broker and deposit bitcoins. Since bitcoins are now generally accepted as a mode of exchange, at least electronically, many brokers are willing to accept them as a currency when you are trading. You will therefore be able to place bitcoins just as you would place dollars in an option investment. You will stand to earn the 70-80% payout if your prediction is right or lose the bitcoins if your prediction was wrong.
2. As an asset – The other option is to trade the bitcoins as an underlying currency. As a binary options trader, you are used to trading on underlying assets such as Google or Amazon stock as well as currencies such as USD/EUR and so on. In these trades, you never buy into the actual shares of the underlying company or had to exchange the actual US dollars with the euros but rather predicted the way their relationship will be. The same story applies with bitcoin. You will predict how it will behave in relation to the US dollar, Canadian dollar, franc or euro.

There are numerous benefits that you will enjoy as a trader once you decide to trade using bitcoin or when you pick it as an underlying currency.

These benefits of using bitcoins in binary option trading are:

1. Bitcoins are decentralized unlike conventional currencies that are controlled centrally. Bitcoins are accessible from anywhere and there is no risk of being told that your bitcoins will only be available as and when the bank has cleared them.

2. Setting up a bitcoin account is easy. All you need to do is access a bitcoin creating computer and start mining your bitcoins. As a binary options trader, you will also find the process of setting up a trading account easy because you can link it easily with your nominal account. This makes it easy for the deposit and withdrawal of your bitcoins to and from the binary options broker's platform.
3. When trading in bitcoins, you will notice that it is quite hard to find it going backwards in value. This means that in most instances, you can rightly predict that a BTC/USD will be bullish and hence place a call trade option. The only thing you need to beware of is to limit how much it can go up in your prediction.

The deposit and withdrawal of bitcoins from your binary options platform is quick and easy, even if some part of the overall system is offline. Moreover, there are no charges relating to bitcoin transactions.

Trading Binary Options Using Bitcoins as Currency

As explained initially, there are basically two ways how this virtual money can be used in binary options trading. The first is to use them as a method of payment when trading binary options. In this case, the virtual currency will act like any other currency such as USD or EUR.

Rather than investing, say, $100 in a binary option contract you may as well invest 10 virtual currencies. Your payout will also be in virtual money. The broker will then transfer the virtual currency to your personal account.

At this moment only a small number of binary options brokers offer Bitcoins as payment and investment method. However, due to the popularity of this virtual money, more and more companies are expected to introduce this form of trading in the future.

The great thing about using this virtual currency in order to make payments at binary options brokers is the fact that you won't have to directly transfer money to a binary broker. You may just exchange USD into Bitcoins and then use the virtual currency to trade binary options. This is completely anonymous.

Trading on the Future Movement of Bitcoins

And the second way in which this virtual currency is used in binary options trading is actually trading on the future movement in the value of Bitcoins. As explained above, each Bitcoin has a value expressed in USD. This value changes all the time depending on how much Bitcoins people buy or sell.

As such, this allows people to trade binary options on Bitcoins. This works the same as trading in the case of any other underlying asset. Imagine the following scenario in order to better understand how this works:

– Currently Bitcoins are priced at $150/coin

– You predict that this will go up to at least $160 in a week

Now, at a Bitcoin binary options broker you will have the possibility to buy a contract that is based on your prediction. Say that you have invested $200 in a contract like this and the broker offered a payout rate of 80%. In case your prediction did indeed come true, then you will receive $360 from the broker.

As said, it's exactly the same as in the case of normal binary options trading.

However, at this moment there are only a very limited number of brokers that offer the possibility to trade on this virtual currency. But experts believe that in the near future trading binary options on Bitcoins will actually be an integral part of the business.

They believe that in a few years there won't be any brokers at all on the market that won't be offering this form of virtual currency. This, however, only under the condition that national governments won't implement laws that would prevent legal binary options brokers from accepting this currency.

As said, governments have no power to shut down Bitcoins however they do have the authority to force licensed operators not to accept this virtual currency. It's not sure at this moment how governments would act once this virtual currency will become even more popular in the future.

Conclusions

Bitcoin is the most popular virtual currency on the Internet at this moment. Due to this and the fact that it can be converted into traditional money (meaning that is has an exchange rate that constantly fluctuates) makes it a viable asset for binary options trading.

However, at this moment only a limited number of brokers accept trading on this virtual currency. But as explained above, this might change soon considering that a significant number of brokers have recently revealed that they are seriously considering implementing this currency.

REFERENCES

CITED ARTICLES

1. S. Nakamoto, "Bitcoin: A Peer-to-Peer Electronic Cash System," 2008.
2. D. Ron and A. Shamir, "How Did Dread Pirate Roberts Acquire and Protect His Bitcoin Wealth?," 2013. [Online]. Available: http://eprint.iacr.org.
3. D. Chaum, "Security Without Identification: Transaction Systems to Make Big Brother Obsolete," vol. 28, no. 10, 1985.
4. Certicom Research, "SEC 2: Recommended Elliptic Curve Domain Parameters," 2010.
5. F. Reid and M. Harrigan, "An Analysis of Anonymity in the Bitcoin System," 2011.
6. E. Androulaki, G. Karame, M. Roeschlin, T. Scherer and S. Capkun, "Evaluating User Privacy in Bitcoin," vol. Financial Cryptography and Data Security, 2013.
7. S. Meiklejohn, M. Pomarole, G. Jordan, K. Levchenko, D. McCoy, G. M. Voelker and S. Savage, "A Fistful of Bitcoins: Characterizing Payments Among Men with No Names," 2013.
8. M. Möser, "Anonymity of Bitcoin Transactions," Münster Bitcoin Conference, 2013.
9. D. Chaum, "Untraceable Electronic Mail, Return Addresses, and Digital Pseudonyms," Commun. ACM, vol. 24, no. 2, pp. 84-88, 1981.

OTHER REFERENCES

- *The Mail Archive post: Bitcoin P2P e-cash paper, accessed 27/01/2014,*
https://www.mailarchive.com/cryptography@metzdowd.com/msg09959.html .

- *Bitcoin open source implementation of P2P currency, accessed 27/01/2014,*

http://p2pfoundation.ning.com/forum/topics/bitcoin-open-source .

- *Portal de Bitcoin, accessed 01/24/2014,* http://www.bitcoin.org .

- *Possible Economic Consequences of Digital Cash, accessed 01/24/2014,*

http://www.isoc.org/inet96/proceedings/b1/b1_1.htm .

- *Bitcoin is evil, accessed 27/01/2014,*
http://krugman.blogs.nytimes.com/2013/12/28/bitcoin-is-evil/

- *La banca china no operará con bitcoins, accessed 01/24/2014,*

http://tecnologia.elpais.com/tecnologia/2013/12/05/actualidad/1386240024_458907.html .

- *eBay to allow Bitcoin sales in 'virtual currency' category, accessed 01/24/2014,*

http://news.cnet.com/8301-1023_3-57617502-93/ebay-to-allow-bitcoin-sales-in-virtual-currencycategory/ .

- *Google Lets Slip That It's Exploring Possible Bitcoin Integration Plans, accessed 01/24/2014,* http://www.forbes.com/sites/andygreenberg/2014/01/22/google-lets-slip-that-its-exploring-possiblebitcoin-integration-plans/ .

- *Application of FinCEN's Regulations to Persons Administering, Exchanging, or Using Virtual Currencies, accessed 01/24/2014,* http://fincen.gov/statutes_regs/guidance/pdf/FIN-2013-G001.pdf.

- *Bitcoin Trade, accessed 01/24/2014,* https://en.bitcoin.it/wiki/Trade .

- *Red Tor: anonimato y vulnerabilidades, accessed 01/24/2014,*

http://inteco.es/blogs/post/Seguridad/BlogSeguridad/Articulo_y_comentarios/red_tor_anonimato_vulnerabilidades .

- *Silk Road: Not Your Father's Amazon.com, accessed 01/24/2014,*

http://www.npr.org/2011/06/12/137138008/silk-road-not-your-fathers-amazon-com .

- *End Of The Silk Road: FBI Says It's Busted The Web's Biggest Anonymous Drug Black Market,accessed 01/24/2014,* http://www.forbes.com/sites/andygreenberg/2013/10/02/end-of-the-silk-roadfbi-busts-the-webs-biggest-anonymous-drug-black-market/ .

www.ingramcontent.com/pod-product-compliance
Lightning Source LLC
Chambersburg PA
CBHW050018230526
45470CB00003B/1026